IT'S TIME TO EAT MONKEY BREAD MUFFINS

It's Time to Eat MONKEY BREAD MUFFINS

Walter the Educator

Silent King Books
A WhichHead Entertainment Imprint

Copyright © 2024 by Walter the Educator

All rights reserved. No part of this book may be reproduced in any manner whatsoever without written per- mission except in the case of brief quotations embodied in critical articles and reviews.

First Printing, 2024

Disclaimer

This book is a literary work; the story is not about specific persons, locations, situations, and/or circumstances unless mentioned in a historical context. Any resemblance to real persons, locations, situations, and/or circumstances is coincidental. This book is for entertainment and informational purposes only. The author and publisher offer this information without warranties expressed or implied. No matter the grounds, neither the author nor the publisher will be accountable for any losses, injuries, or other damages caused by the reader's use of this book. The use of this book acknowledges an understanding and acceptance of this disclaimer.

It's Time to Eat MONKEY BREAD MUFFINS is a collectible early learning book by Walter the Educator suitable for all ages belonging to Walter the Educator's Time to Eat Book Series. Collect more books at WaltertheEducator.com

USE THE EXTRA SPACE TO TAKE NOTES AND DOCUMENT YOUR MEMORIES

MONKEY BREAD MUFFINS

Wake up, wake up, it's time for a treat,

It's Time to Eat

Monkey Bread Muffins

A warm little muffin that's sticky and sweet.

Monkey Bread Muffins, fresh from the pan,

Let's grab one quick, oh, yes, we can!

Cinnamon sugar swirls all around,

Pull them apart, they're soft and round.

Each little piece is gooey and yum,

Perfect for nibbling on fingers and thumb.

The smell fills the air, it's oh-so-nice,

Like sugar and cinnamon mixed with spice.

Hot from the oven, be careful, take care,

Wait just a moment, they're worth the share!

Take a big bite, oh, what a surprise,

The sweetness and butter will light up your eyes.

Sticky on fingers, but that's okay,

Monkey Bread Muffins will brighten your day!

It's Time to Eat Monkey Bread Muffins

Roll up the dough, piece by piece,

Dip it in butter for a sugary feast.

Pop it in pans, let it bake so slow,

Watch as they rise, all golden aglow!

They're perfect for breakfast or snack time fun,

Monkey Bread Muffins are loved by everyone.

Pass them around, they're soft and warm,

A muffin hug is their special charm.

Add raisins or nuts, or leave them plain,

Each tiny bite is like sunshine, not rain.

Drizzle some glaze or eat them as they are,

Monkey Bread Muffins are snack-time stars!

Pull-apart fun with each little piece,

Eating these muffins feels like a feast.

Soft in the middle and sweet on the top,

It's Time to Eat

Monkey Bread Muffins

You'll keep on munching, you just can't stop!

Share with your family, share with your friends,

Monkey Bread Muffins bring joy that never ends.

Take one, take two, but leave some behind,

Sharing is caring, and that's always kind!

So next time you smell that cinnamon breeze,

And hear the sizzle that puts you at ease,

Know it's a moment to gather and grin,

It's Time to Eat Monkey Bread Muffins

Monkey Bread Muffins are ready, dig in!

ABOUT THE CREATOR

Walter the Educator is one of the pseudonyms for Walter Anderson. Formally educated in Chemistry, Business, and Education, he is an educator, an author, a diverse entrepreneur, and he is the son of a disabled war veteran. "Walter the Educator" shares his time between educating and creating. He holds interests and owns several creative projects that entertain, enlighten, enhance, and educate, hoping to inspire and motivate you. Follow, find new works, and stay up to date with Walter the Educator™

at WaltertheEducator.com

www.ingramcontent.com/pod-product-compliance
Lightning Source LLC
LaVergne TN
LVHW052013060526
838201LV00059B/4010